Kingston a... :on
— Ol... ...

C000128803

Thames Street has existed since early medieval times. By the 19th century it was an important shopping centre, often called "The Bond Street of Surrey". This view is looking north to the junction with Clarence Street. On the right hand corner of the junction is a distant view of the Kingston Gas Co. offices. On the left hand corner is David Atkins celebrated bakery and Scotch Cafe. This picture must have been taken before 1912 because that was the year the Blue Anchor closed. This 200-year-old pub on the right, with

Kingston-on-Thames, Thames Street
(Publ: anon. 573. Postally unused.)

the horse-van parked outside, was then converted into a shop and its upper frontage, heavily "Tudorised", still survives.

The shop on the left, (above) with the striped blind, is that of Henry White, the school and college outfitter. Next door, at number 11, is Funston Benson, the trunk and bag maker. One firm still survives in Thames Street from Victorian times: The Jewellers and Silversmiths Co. Ltd., at No. 15.

June Sampson

ACKNOWLEDGEMENTS

This book could not have materialised without unstinting help
from many people.

Special thanks go to Tony Durrant and Stephen Day, whose idea it was,
who cajoled and encouraged, and who showed great skill and daring in
taking the contemporary photographs in the teeth of today's traffic.

Great gratitude must go to Anne McCormack, archivist to the Royal
Borough, and to Anne Baker, Tim Everson and Simon Davies
of Kingston Museum and Heritage Centre.
Their patience never falters in the face of my incessant demands.

My thanks, too, to Martin Higgins of Kingston Planning Department,
for assisting so willingly in the often complex problem of discovering
building dates.

The publishers wish to thank Les Kirkin for his continuing help, advice
and skill in making prints of to-day's scenes from our negatives.

Our thanks are also due to Mr & Mrs L. King of Tolworth
for the use of the postcard of Tolworth Rise on page 76,
and to Henry Scott of Surbiton for the picture
of The Waggon & Horses on page 55.

**First published and © 1992 by
Marine Day Publishers
64 Cotterill Road, Surbiton KT6 7UN
Surrey.
Tel: 081 399 7625**

All rights reserved. No part of this publication may be reproduced, stored in a retrieval system,
or transmitted in any form without permission of the publisher.

ISBN 0 9516076 2 6 Kingston and Surbiton — Old & New (pbk)

Printed and bound for The Marine Press Ltd.
by Alderson Brothers Printers Ltd., Hersham, Surrey.

CONTENTS

INTRODUCTION

If you were marooned on a desert island, what luxury would you choose to have with you? We all know, and have probably pondered, that famous question from BBC Radio's Desert Island Discs programme. I'm pretty sure of my answer. It would, I think, have to be my collection of old local postcard views.

Perhaps "collection" is too grand a word for my random heaps, stored higgledy-piggledy in an assortment of plastic carrier bags so I can tip them instantly on to the nearest table to be gloated and pored over. But they give me such pleasure that this book nearly didn't happen.

Yes, I was flattered beyond measure when Marine Day Publishers, in the persons of Tony Durrant and Stephen Day, asked me to write it. They are among the few publishers of local history whose standards I truly respect, and I wanted my name to be associated with theirs. Then I realised it would mean parting with my postcards, certainly for weeks, and possibly for months, while contemporary photographs of the same scenes were taken, and the book was designed, typeset and so on. It was such a dismal prospect that I was tempted to abandon the project altogether. Finally common sense prevailed. Even so, the pain when I had to relinquish them, and my joy when we were eventually re-united, was so great that Messrs Durrant and Day must privately have thought me deranged.

The fact is, though, that vintage postcard views can easily become an addiction, particularly when they're of places one is deeply involved in.

My collection is devoted entirely to the Royal borough of Kingston upon Thames, where I came to live 30 years ago. In those days it was still Kingston-on-Thames, and Surbiton and New Malden could still glory in their hard-won independence as separate boroughs, each with its own civic structure, arms and regalia. Then came the massive local government re-organisation of 1965. Surbiton and New Malden were reluctantly merged with Kingston to form the new borough of Kingston upon Thames.

The place has lost a lot more than its hyphens since then. Indeed, it has altered so much that in many areas it bears no resemblance at all to what I saw and fell in love with three decades ago. I love it still, but with increasing feelings of anger and regret at what is being done to it.

Of course, change is inevitable. Of course, towns must adjust to life as it is now instead of endlessly looking back to a past that probably wasn't nearly as golden at the time as it seems to have been now. But it is possible to effect these changes without destroying the individuality and ambience that make ancient towns like Kingston so special.

Bath and Cambridge have managed it, for example, whereas Oxford and Bristol have not. Neither, I fear, has Kingston. Look at what's been done to the historic Horsefair area. Look at the newly brutalised approach into the town from Kingston Bridge. Look at the ruthless architecture of Kingston College of Further Education, Kingston Hospital and other major buildings which, because of their size and position, dominate the whole townscape. Consider the ugliness and ill-judged layout of some parts of the long-awaited town centre relief road, and the policy of centering so much on the Clarence Street area to the detriment of other thoroughfares. All of these changes — and there are plenty more to come — make me treasure my postcards the more.

When I first began acquiring them it was as a casual, mildly enjoyable pastime that confirmed that Kingston hadn't really changed that much. Now, bearing out the old maxim that you don't fully appreciate anything until it's gone, postcards from the past have become my passion, re-creating landmarks I once knew.

Often they're the work of the best photographers and artists of the day, people who really knew and loved the area, and could capture its atmosphere. Thus, some of the pictures are so alive you can, figuratively speaking, step into them and feel you're part of the scene. That's what I do, finding fresh details to exclaim over and research every time.

Clearly I'm not alone in this. Old topographical postcards, once a minority and blissfully cheap interest, are now so popular that cards that cost me pence a few years ago are now priced at several pounds.

Not that I'm interested in cash gain. I choose a view for its own sake, regardless of whether its a commonplace mass production or a rare collector's item; and the pleasure I get from each never lessens, no matter how often I look at them.

This book will, I hope, give you something of the same feeling if you haven't already experienced it.

My love affair with postcards has one condition: they must be the genuine vintage article and not one of the modern reproductions now so readily available. These are very good, of course, and can tell you a lot. But they simply don't have the same special magic as a veteran card with, ideally, postmark and message still intact.

The idea of a card that could be sent through the post with no need for an envelope seems so simple that it's surprising the first one was not issued until October 1869 in Austria. Britain followed exactly a year later with a card pre-printed with a halfpenny stamp, ready for sending.

These were not picture postcards, but plain rectangles, with the stamp and address on one side and the other left blank for messages. Only in 1894 did the British Post Office permit the picture cards that had been popular in Europe for the previous 22 years. However, in 1902 Britain was the first country to issue picture postcards with a divided back, enabling the message to be written on the same side as the address. Previous to that, the message had to be crammed into a tiny blank space alongside the picture.

This simple innovation opened the floodgates, and soon more than 860 million cards were being posted in Britain every year. As a card could be posted and delivered on the same day, they were used much as telephones are today.

Collecting them also became the vogue, with most households owning special albums in which to paste them. The postcard heyday lasted until the outbreak of World War 1. Since then, though they have remained popular, they have never again become a huge national craze.

June Sampson

POPULATION

M.B. — Municipal Borough   (*1991 Census figures not yet published)   U.D. — Urban District

YEAR	KINGSTON	SURBITON
1841	9,760	387
1851	12,144	2,800
1861	17,792	-
1871	27,073	-
1881	35,829	5,569
1891	44,237	5,710
1901	54,119 (M.B. 34,375)	15,017
1911	M.B. 37,975	U.D. 17,717 } includes Hook,
1921	M.B. 39,514	U.D. 19,547 } Tolworth and
1931	M.B. 39,825	U.D. 29,401 } Southborough
1941	No Census	No Census
1951	M.B. 40,172	M.B. 60,875
1981*	Kingston + N.Kingston+New Malden 22,808 20,957 27,090 **Total:** 70,855	Surbiton+Tolworth+Chess'ton+W.Park 22,898 17,114 20,281 4,936 **Total:** 65,229

Original Publishers of the Postcards — some notes and dates

A.S. Series. — This was possibly the Artistic Stationery Company which provided both print and photographic cards over many years from the early 1900's.

Balmer, Kingston. — *S.J.Balmer, Stationers of 51 Kingston Hill.* This local retailer traded from 1912—1928. *(Kelly's)*

Boots Cash Chemist & Boots Pure Drug Co. Ltd. — The original chemist shop opened by Jesse Boot in 1850, was in his home town of Nottingham. However, the earliest Boots postcard found has an 1899 postmark. The small circular Pelham Series trade mark is shown on most postcards, but in 1914 another mark was registered with a large letter "B" in the centre, and later still came the trade mark showing the familiar full name.

Bull & Son, Surbiton. —The earliest reference found for this company was in 1865 at 20, Victoria Road. The firm is listed only as *bookbinders* in 1890, but from the turn of the century it had developed into a full bookbinding, bookseller's, printer's and stationer's business. This lasted until 1915, when only the latter two trades are listed. They still operate a stationers shop at 21 Victoria Road to-day. *(Phillipson's & Kelly's Directories)*

Collectors' Publishing Co. — *42/44 Imperial Buildings, Ludgate Circus, London. E.C.* This was one of the largest distributors/agents for topographical postcards for S.W. London. It originally had offices in Fleet Street and the Company was active between 1901 and 1907. Their "Mercury" series was the name printed on cards issued by the firm, to distinguish their *own* publications from others they handled.

Frith F. & Co. Ltd. Reigate. Surrey. — The original Francis Frith was born in 1822 in Chesterfield. An unsuccessful wholesale grocer he turned to printing in 1850, and thence to photography. By 1859 he had established a new business in Reigate. Following successful publication of books of photographs of his personal foreign travels, the Reigate firm became the largest photographic distributors in the world. His two sons gradually took over the business which became a Limited Company in 1896. Most of the 'Frith Series' postcards were printed after the first World War when Frith's grandson, Francis E. Frith joined the company. The company was sold as recently as 1968 but went into liquidation in 1971. By this time the archive contained photos of over 4000 British cities, towns and villages and was saved from destruction when bought by Rothmans Intenational. The present day Company, *The Francis Frith Collection PLC*, started in 1977, following the purchase of the archive from Rothmans. To-day, the business publishes Frith photographs for sale by mail order and in over 1000 shops throughout Britain

The Morland Studio, Kingston. —Started in 1907 at 21 Market Place; then by 1908 had moved to Clarence Street, and is listed at No 36 between 1908 and 1911. From 1918, until 1925 when the firm is no longer shown, the address given is 17 Clarence Street. *(Kelly's; & Professional Photographers in Kingston 1854—1911. RPS & Heritage Centre)*

Oak Cabin Series — The 'Oak Cabin' was the shop at Tolworth Rise which sold a series of local postcards of around the 1930's era. The name survives today over the newsagents shop on the A3 at Tolworth Rise. (see page 76)

Photochrom Co. Ltd. Tunbridge Wells. —One of the most prolific postcard publishers of them all had Swiss origins, around 1894. Although the premises for the London company were at 61 and 63 Ludgate Hill, the principals, Messrs F. & A. Wilde, who were both lithographers, lived in Tunbridge Wells. The Photochrom Company Ltd., registered in Great Britain in December 1896, quickly expanded and a year later its offices were moved to 121 Cheapside; moving yet again later on to 35/36 Hosier Lane, Snow Hill E.C. remaining there for many years.

Raphael Tuck & Sons Ltd. —This name stands foremost in the history of Fine Art Publishing in Great Britain. Quality, leadership and creativity were associated with this Company at a time of strong continental competition (although Raphael Tuch was himself a Prussian Jew who came to London in 1865). 14 pages of Company history cover this entry right up to the present day, but with greater detail covering the years 1900-1914.

Rotary Photo E.C. —One of the largest of the Real Photo. postcard publishers. Took its name from the use of rotary presses to produce cards at its works in West Drayton, circa 1900. By 1904 the monthly output of cards was 250,000.

Russell, Surbiton. —Frank and Frederick Russell had their photographic business at 7, Lower Brighton Terrace, Surbiton, between 1895 and 1908 *(Professional Photographers in Kingston 1854—1911. RPS & Heritage Centre)*

Seymour, T. Hook Rd. Surbiton. —This was Thomas Seymour, whose newsagent's business is listed from 1910 to 1935. From 1922 the full address of 152 Hook Road, Surbiton is given. *(Kelly's Directories)*

Stengel & Co. Ltd. London E.C. —A German firm based in Dresden and Berlin. By 1902 could offer 10,000 different topographical cards covering most parts of Europe, Middle East, Russia, Japan and Australia. The Dresden works employed 250 people and produced 30 million postcards each year. In 1901, the Company's British agent O. Flammger was appointed and his initials appear in front of the Company name on many cards.

Valentine & Sons Ltd. Dundee. —Another giant in the postcard world from the early days until the 1960's, claiming a history of well over 50 years, including being the first publisher to introduce cards where the picture entirely covered the front (i.e. borderless) around 1902. Also, patented in 1906, was the novelty postcard called *The Kissogram,* where the sender recorded his kiss on a blank square from an 'impression' taken from large red lips impregnated with colour and printed elsewhere on the card. Five pages of Company history form this entry.

(References to non-local publishers taken from 'Picture Postcards and their Publishers' by Anthony Byatt)

Kingston Upon Thames

The photographer is looking west down East Lane to High Street. The timbered building on the left dates from the mid-1500's and is the oldest surviving domestic architecture in Kingston. Originally it was a single house of great quality, probably built for one of Kingston's many prosperous merchants. However, by the 19th century it had been converted into three shops —37, 39, and 41 — with living accommodation over. At the time this picture was taken, and for many years before and after that, 37 was occupied by Wilcox & Son, noted butchers who supplied the Royal family with meat when they were at Claremont, Esher.

A Bit of Old Kingston-on-Thames.
(Publ: Boots Cash Chemist — 'Real Photograph' series. Postally unused.)

Equally long-standing tenants, at 39, were the Mould family, boat builders and proprietors, who claimed to have built and launched Kingston's first steam vessel. In recent years the building has been restored throughout to a very high standard. Now the whole of 41 and the ground floor of 39 is occupied by Pizza Express.

Coronation Stone. Kingston.   *(Publ: anon. Postally used 1904.)*

The Coronation Stone, on which seven Saxon kings are said to have been crowned, was rescued from obscurity in 1850 and, with much ceremony, placed in a prominent spot near the junction of Kingston Market Place and Eden Street.   On the right are the premises of Cresswell Ball & Co., piano tuners, and W.Brewster the chemist, who proudly proclaims in large letters that he is patronised by the Royal Family.   Further along is the dominating sign of Drewett & Sons, printers. The firm changed to Knapp Drewett & Sons in 1900, indicating that the picture was taken before the turn of the century.   The Brewster and Cresswell Ball shops have long since been demolished and replaced by a bank. The Griffin Hotel, on the left, had a history stretching back to Tudor times. Its frontage still survives, but the building has been converted into a shopping complex known as Griffin Walk. The Coronation Stone was moved to the south side of the Guildhall in 1935.

The Market, Kingston-on-Thames. *(Publ: M.J.R. B. — M.J.Ridley, Bournemouth. 7220. Postally used 1908.)*
This picture must have been taken prior to 1900 because early in the year Drewett & Sons, whose sign is prominently displayed on the right, changed its name to Knapp Drewett & Sons following the merger of Mary Anne Knapp's *Surrey Comet* newspaper and printing operation with William Drewett's *Kingston and Surbiton News* and printing business. To the left of what was then the Guildhall, but is now the Market House, are the mid-19th century shops that in 1909 were given a lavishly ornate mock-Tudor facade by Boots the chemists. Horse transport and cycles were still undisturbed by the internal combustion engine at this time. However, over the decades the Market Place became increasingly hazardous to pedestrians as cars and buses used its west side as a main road linking Portsmouth Road with Thames Street and Kingston Bridge. This ended in 1989, with the completion of the town centre relief road and the re-routing of all town centre traffic. So the Market Place is no longer a through-way.

Kingston-on-Thames, The Market. *(Publ: anon. L.L. No. 571)*

The top-hatted coachman and the elegant lady pedestrian in the left foreground indicate that this picture was taken in the morning, when the upper classes visited the market. The middle orders went there in the afternoon, while the poorest waited until the evening, when remaining stocks were sold off cheaply. The car parked on the extreme right gives a hint of the road revolution to come. The building to the left of the Guildhall still awaits its mock-Tudor encrustation, indicating that the picture was taken before 1909. The little 16th century building next door is still Ye Olde Segar Shoppe, run by Nuthalls. Later it was acquired by Boots. Now, together with the shops adjoining, it is a branch of the Next fashion chain. The statue and drinking fountain, which survives today, is a memorial to Henry Shrubsole, who was serving his third consecutive term as Mayor of Kingston when he died suddenly in 1880 while distributing gifts to the aged poor.

The Market Place, Kingston-on-Thames *(Publ: Valentine's Series. Postally unused.)*

The uniformed officer walking smartly down the centre of the Market Place suggests this was taken during the 1914-18 War. Cars are a rapidly expanding presence, but still share the highway with elegant horse-drawn vehicles. Boots have now applied their mock-Tudor facade and gables to the buildings left of the Guildhall. Mock-Tudor beams have also been superimposed onto the authentic Tudor shop next door! The church clock shows it is 11.30 a.m. so the better-off townspeople are still doing their morning shopping when produce is at its freshest and prices at their highest. In 1985 the Market Place was pedestrianised on its north and east sides. However, since 1989 drivers have been confronted by a puzzling sign that reads: *Market Area Closed to all Vehicles. Access permitted except Mon., Tues., Thurs., Fri., 10.30 a.m. to 4 p.m. Sat., 10.00 a.m. to 5.00 p.m.* It takes some working out!

Market Place, Kingston-on-Thames. *(Publ: Valentine's Series. Postally used 1905.)*

Only in comparatively recent times has Kingston Market operated on six days a week. Previously trading was confined to Wednesdays, Thursdays and Saturdays and stalls were dismantled after use. Hence the uncharacteristically spacious view seen here. This picture is unusual in that it clearly shows the buildings on the east side of the Market Place. The one with the twin gables and the window boxes is The Wheatsheaf, a 17th century inn frequented by Charles Dickens. Next door but two, with a single gable, is the Coach and Horses, an ancient pub noted as a meeting place for bare-knuckle fighters. The Wheatsheaf closed in 1961 and was converted into a shop (now Rymans). Its upper facade remains. The east side of Market Place was known as Cook Row in medieval times because it specialised in food shops. That tradition is still maintained by Dewhurst the Butcher, and The Bakers Oven, who sell bread and cakes in what was once Alfred Emms saddlery, patronised by the Empress Eugenie.

The Old Apple Market c1900.   *(Publ: anon. Postally unused.)*

The Apple Market has existed in Kingston town centre since medieval times. The ancient timbered building to the left, beyond the fruit and vegetable stalls, was the Old Harrow. It had been an inn since the early 16th century when it was abruptly closed by the licensing magistrates in 1912. It was then converted into shops by raising the upper floor and keeping it suspended while the ground floor was rebuilt. It was then eased back into position. Thus there are some genuine old timbers concealed behind the pseudo-antique frontage we see now. To-day the erstwhile Old Harrow is the home of the Market Bakery, Watts Radio and Markew Bros., the butchers. The former shop of the leading drapers, Hancock & Baker, is now the home of the Health Food Shop, with offices above. On the right is The Apple Market pub, known as The Morning Star when the postcard picture was taken.

Kingston-on-Thames. High Street. *(Publ: Photochrom Co. Ltd. No. 80689. Postally used 1939)*

One of the greatest townscape tragedies of post-war Kingston was the destruction of the ancient gabled building on the right. It was originally The Crane, an inn where ambassadors and members of the royal court often lodged when the monarch was at Hampton Court Palace. Later it was the Parliamentarians' county military HQ during the Civil Wars of the 17th century. Throughout the 19th century it was known as the Jolly Butcher. In 1912 Hodgsons' Kingston Brewery's lease on the building expired. It then became a popular restaurant, Ye Olde Post House, on the upper floors and Wrathall's celebrated Old Curiosity Shop at ground level. In 1954 the building was destroyed to make way for shops and offices. Beyond Clattern Bridge is the fine white facade of the Odeon Cinema, opened in 1933 as one of the first three Odeons in Britain. It was demolished in 1988, and the site is now a car park pending redevelopment. Further along the street, as it curves to the left, is the chimney and distinctive outline of the Eagle Brewery. This closed in the 1920's but part of its street frontage has been retained.

The "New Bentalls"   *(Publ: Anon. Postally unused.)*

Leonard Bentall had a grand design: to rebuild his family's department store with an unbroken facade stretching 700 feet along Wood Street and curving round the corner into Clarence Street. He was also adamant that the facade be modelled on the William and Mary wing of Hampton Court Palace, designed by Sir Christopher Wren. Building work began in 1930 and the first Wood Street section was opened on 19th November, 1931. The second phase, including the dramatic curve into Clarence Street, was begun in 1934. Its completion was celebrated on 9th Sept. 1935, when trumpeters of the Coldstream Guards stood in full ceremonial dress on the large canopy overhanging the ground floor corner windows. Here they performed a fanfare at hourly intervals, bringing traffic to a standstill as crowds packed the road to listen. This artist's representation shows Leonard Bentall's original scheme. However, the curving corner section eventually took a different form as shown below in 1964.

Clarence Street, Kingston-on-Thames. *(Publ: F.Frith & Co., Ltd. No. F.U.S./KTN 59. Postally unused.)*
"That's because at the start of the scheme Wood Street was a very narrow, secondary thoroughfare, and my father envisaged the main entrance being on the Clarence Street corner," explained Mr Rowan Bentall, who is President of Bentalls. "Then Wood Street was widened into a dual carriageway to encourage traffic to avoid the congestion of Clarence Street and allow kerbside parking in Wood Street. So the main entrance was sited in Wood Street instead." This view, looking east up Clarence Street was taken in 1959. Three decades later all the buildings on both sides as far as Bentalls have been demolished. Those on the left went to make way for the town centre relief road and the John Lewis department store, opened in 1990. Those on the right were replaced by new shops and offices. Bentalls facade still dominates the junction with Wood Street, but the department store that existed behind it was demolished in 1990 and replaced by the Bentall Centre. This contains a hundred retail units, and opened in 1992.

Clarence Street, Kingston on Thames. *(Publ: F.Frith. No. KTN. 107. Postally unused.)*
This view dates from the early 1960's, but all the buildings survive with the exception of Bentalls on the left. This was demolished in 1990 to be replaced by the Bentall Centre, a palatial shopping mall developed by Norwich Union in conjunction with Bentalls. It contains 100 shop units, and its most spectacular feature is a barrel-vaulted atrium, 100feet high and 400 feet long. Clarence Street was originally a modest thoroughfare named Norbiton Street. It gained a new name and status when it became the approach road to the handsome new Kingston Bridge, opened by the Duchess of Clarence in 1828. The most striking change to Clarence Street since the 1960's is the disappearance of traffic. The road was pedestrianised in 1989, following completion of the town centre relief road. The Bentall Centre was in the final stage of construction when this picture was taken, and the attendant screens and barriers seriously restrict the view of the street. However, the shot should prove interesting to historians of the future.

Canbury Gardens, Kingston-on-Thames. *(Publ: anon. Postally used — no postmark.)*

Canbury Gardens, seen here looking south, has been a popular riverside amenity in Kingston ever since it opened in 1890. For centuries it had been an isolated stretch of swamps and osier beds. Then, following the post-railway building boom, it became a foul rubbish dump. A few public-spirited people campaigned to have the land reclaimed and laid out as a much-needed public garden. Eventually, in August 1889, work began on constructing the first thousand feet, starting from Down Hall Road. The rest of the gardens, and the two riverside walks, were completed in stages over the rest of the decade. In 1891 a prominent townsman, Charles Nuthall, presented the gardens with a handsome bandstand, which cost the then large sum of "between two and three hundred pounds", and was copied from one in Hamburg. Thereafter music concerts were a regular attraction until the bandstand was removed to provide metal for wartime munitions. The chimney seen rising above the trees on the left belonged to

Canbury Gardens, Kingston-on-Thames. *(Publ: Bentalls Kingston-on-Thames Series. Postally unused.)*
*(from p. 18)*the Native Guano Works, where Kingston's raw sewage was dried in great ovens and converted into garden fertiliser — emanating an odour which sent people fleeing from Canbury Gardens each time there was a baking session! **(Above)** Canbury Gardens a decade or two later, looking north towards Richmond. The towpath and promenade survive unscathed to-day, as does the fine row of London plane trees planted in the early 1900's. The major change is in the landscaping. Until the 1950's, Canbury Gardens featured formal flower beds, shrubberies and grass verges, as seen on the right. Then Kingston Corporation changed its landscaping policy, and began replacing flower beds with open greensward, so people could sit and stroll more freely. The main horticultural nurseries for the old Royal Borough of Kingston were in Canbury Gardens for many years, on what is now the site of the Tennis Centre. The early 1970's saw their transfer to a new location in Old Tolworth Road.

Skating Rink, Kingston. *(Publ: A.S. Series No. 33. Postally unused.)*

Kingston Skating Rink opened in Canbury Park Road in September 1909 when a craze for roller skating was at its height. Three years later its popularity had waned, and the Rink was rented to the famous pioneer airman, Tom Sopwith. Here he established his Sopwith Aviation Co. and produced a famous range of bi-planes, notably the revolutionary Tabloid. This was built in strict secrecy in the Rink, its design chalked out on the 16,000 square feet of polished wood floor where countless Kingstonians had previously fallen flat on their faces. After World War I, Sopwith moved to large, purpose-built premises in Canbury Park Road, and the Rink was re-opened to skaters. The advertisement below is from the *Surrey Comet* of 24th December 1910 and shows the range of entertainment offered by The Rink, which adjoined the Cinem Palace. This was later rebuilt as the Regal Cinema and still survives as the Gala Bingo Club. The Rink building was demolished in the 1980's to make way for an office development.

THE RINK,

(Adjoining Cinem Palace)

KINGSTON STATION. Tel. 228 Kingston.

Special Attractions during Xmas Week.

FULL MILITARY BAND.

MONDAY & TUESDAY, 26TH & 27TH — THREE SESSIONS DAILY—
MORNING, 10—1 ; AFTERNOON, 3—5.30 ; EVENING, 7.30—11.

WEDNESDAY EVENING, 28TH — **SPORTS ON WHEELS.**
Including Team Race ;   Richmond R.S.C. and Kingston R.S.C.
Musical Chairs and Searching for the South Pole.
The Evening will conclude with a GRAND CONFETTI BATTLE, at which
all are invited to take part.

THURSDAY AFTERNOON, 29TH — RACES FOR CHILDREN, UNDER 14,
Girls Balloon and Hoop Race.   Boys One-Legged and Potato Race.
Special Attractions for Evening—See Handbills.   Entries to all events, Wednesday
and Thursday, FREE, and numbers limited.   Prizes will be given.
Entries to be made to the Manager, before the commencement of sports.

FRIDAY AFTERNOON, 30TH — Special Go-as-you-Please turns for Children,
at which all will be admitted FREE.

SATURDAY, 31ST — Make a Good Finish by Skating the Old Year out at the
Popular Rink — Prices as Usual.

DON'T FORGET, HOCKEY MATCH, Kingston *v*. Richmond, TO-NIGHT, AT 9.

Regatta, Kingston-on-Thames   *(Publ: Valentine's Series No. 07443. Postally used 1909.)*

Kingston had an annual Royal regatta long before the celebrated event at Henley. It was Kingston Watermen's Regatta, launched and paid for by Queen Adelaide early in the 1820's, and open to everyone employed on the river at Kingston and Hampton Wick. It was always held on August 18th, the Queen's birthday. Several other regattas came later, including Kingston Regatta, established in 1857; Kingston Town Regatta, launched by local tradesmen in 1865; Kingston Borough Regatta, inaugurated in 1890 and Teddington Reach Regatta, organised by Kingston Skiff Club. In 1869 Kingston Town Regatta became the first to include fireworks and a display of illuminated boats on the Thames. It was such a resounding success that the idea was copied by clubs up and down the country, and transformed regattas from a specialists' pastime to a hugely popular public diversion. Of all these events, only Kingston Regatta survives. It is organised by Kingston Rowing Club and is still going strong after 135 years.

Acre Road, Kingston. *(Publ: anon. Real Photograph. Postally used 1907.)*

Forty Acres was a lane, running east from Richmond Road alongside open fields. For generations it marked the end of the town, and there was no street lighting beyond it. The opening of Kingston Station in 1863 brought huge changes as the fields bordering Richmond Road swiftly filled with streets and houses. By 1868, Forty Acres had become Acre Road, a street of modest houses, occupied by houses designed for the so-called "labouring classes". In this picture a horse-drawn delivery cart has stopped outside The Lamb beerhouse, and the road is like a self-contained village with its own fishmonger, bootmaker, baker and greengrocer. Today the north side of the road is relatively unscathed, but the south side is much changed. The Lamb, now a fully fledged pub visible just beyond the lamp-post, was re-fronted several years ago. The cottages running from The Lamb to Cowleaze Road were demolished to provide a car park for the Knitmaster factory in Cowleaze Road. Waights Court, one of three blocks of flats built between 1961 and 1965 is named after the Waight family, who ran a dairy farm on this site for 160 years.

King's Road, Kingston-on-Thames. *(Publ: O.F. [Stengal & Co., Ltd] Postally used 1909.)*

Until the 1860's, King's Road was a quiet country route, known as The Kings Highway. It ran through open fields to link Richmond Road with the Kingston gates to Richmond Park, and probably got its old name because it was maintained by the Crown. After the opening of Kingston Station in 1863, many acres of ancient farmland were bought up for housing. The Kings Highway was then adopted by the local authority, widened and re-named King's Road. This part of it survives virtually unchanged save for the disappearance of trams, tramlines and the graceful street lamps; and the shop on the left continued its long career as a family butcher until recent times. Now it is being used as offices. The modern view, looking east from Acre Road, features roadworks on the right of the junction. The completed result is, to quote the latest local government jargon, a "traffic calming device" — in other words a raised strip which protrudes into the road to force vehicles to slow down on the bend.

Kingston Infirmary.   *(Publ. anon. Postally unused)*

This was Kingston Union Workhouse male infirmary, designed by W.H.Hope and built in 1897 for the then large sum of £18,000.

During World War I it treated military casualties so successfully that it was allowed to change its name to Kingston and District Hospital. This greatly boosted morale because the word "infirmary" was synonymous with the workhouse, so rousing strong public prejudice. The building now forms part of Kingston Hospital and the exterior, with its careful brick detailing, survives virtually unchanged. The only casualty is the balconied section, which was bombed in World War II and replaced by the ugly infill that now houses the surgical day unit.

The central tower originally held a reserve water tank, placed high enough to serve all parts of the building. Now it serves as a lift shaft.

Nurses Home, Kingston Hill. *(Publ: A.S. No. 727. Postally used 1928)*

An excited young nurse sent this card to her family in Bedfordshire soon after Kingston and District Hospital's new nurses home had been formally opened by the Duchess of York in 1928. "What do you think of this big house? It is where I live and I have got a dear little bedroom all to myself," she wrote. A hint of duty hours is given in her next sentence: "I will come home and see you when I get my day off next month." The hospital at this time was still administered by the Poor Law Guardians of the Kingston Union, and formed part of the workhouse complex on Kingston Hill. The new nurses home, along with other improvements, were essential because of the increasing number of cases being handled by the hospital. For example, in 1914 the hospital treated 1,543 patients, carried out 85 major operations and had a nursing staff of 67. In 1927, the year work began on the new building, there were 3,521 patients, 348 major operations and a nursing staff of 109. The building was designed by architect F. Danby Smith, and the exterior remains the same today.

Kingston Hill. (Publ: Phillipson's Press Ltd., St James' Road Kingston-on-Thames. Postally unused)
This picture is interesting in that it shows a centuries-old mode of public transport sharing the highway with what was then the latest development in travel technology. Coming down the Hill is a horse-drawn vehicle of the type that had made Kingston famous as a coaching centre since the 18th century. Following close behind is one of the electric tram cars, introduced to Kingston with much ceremony on 1st March 1906 (an event sadly marred on Kingston Hill, when a brewery drayhorse took fright, collided with the inaugural tram and hurled the managing director of London United Transport, Sir Clifton Robertson, into the road. He never fully recovered from the shock of the fall). The shops on the left are the same as those shown opposite. Beyond them, on the corner of Queen's Road, is the Albert Hotel named after the Prince-Consort. Edward VII was an occasional visitor here. In 1988 the Albert, which had been ruthlessly modernised over the years, was expensively refurbished and restored to Victorian style.

Norbiton, Kingston Hill.   *(Publ: T.S.Mansfield, Norbiton. Postally used 1910.)*

Kingston Hill looking towards Kingston town centre in about 1907. The horse-drawn cart in the right foreground waits outside the grocery shop run by Henry Minnitt, who came to Kingston as a humble shop assistant in the 1870's and ultimately became one of the most prominent men in Edwardian Kingston. He even made national headlines when he became the first man to be elected Mayor of Kingston three years in succession, serving from 1903. He died in 1914 but his shop, established in 1890, still survives as Oddbins and is virtually unchanged, inside and out, on the upper floors. Nearby shops include Eckford's Bakery, Frank Bastable, fishmonger, and Money Bros. dairymen. The tower further down the hill is that of Kingston Methodist Church built in 1886, and demolished in 1959 to be replaced by offices. The horse-drawn van on the left is part of the delivery fleet of the South Western Sanitary Laundry, which opened in 1872 in what were then the rural fields of Oil Mill Lane — later re-named Villiers Road.

Crescent Road, Kingston Hill. *(Publ: Balmer, Kingston. Postally unused.)*

Though Crescent Road was constructed in 1854, it took more than 50 years to fill it with houses. This view looks west from Kingston Hill towards Queen's Road. Behind the fences on the left and right are the large gardens of The Grange and The Knowle respectively. The last great stately home to be built in Kingston was constructed on the north side of Crescent Road in 1914. It was Kingsnympton Hall, set in 20 acres of parkland with lakes, woodland, tiered Italian and old English gardens and a swimming pool built entirely of Carrara marble. The house was bombed in 1940. Early in the 1950s Malden and Coombe Council joined forces with Kingston to buy the site and re-develop it as Kingsnympton council estate. The impressive entrance gate pillars of the hall still survive. They are just out of sight, to the right foreground of this picture.

Queen's Road, Kingston-on-Thames. *(Publ: O.F. [Stengel & Co. Ltd.] Postally unused.)*

In 1853 the National Land Society bought 54 acres on Kingston Hill and immediately began laying out roads and selling plots to their shareholders for the building of middle and upper class houses. The first roads to be constructed included Queen's Road and Crescent Road (*see page 28*) which were both laid out in 1854.

This view looks towards Richmond Park, whose gates are visible in the distance. On the left is Tudor Road.

In 1931 the residents, determined to preserve their leafy peace, managed to fight off plans to route trolley buses along Queen's Road. Now, however, the thoroughfare is heavily used by traffic to and from the park and many of the elegant houses have given way to flats.

Kingston Hill. *(Publ: anon. Postally unused.)*

Though this card is labelled Kingston Hill, it should strictly speaking be London Road as Kingston Hill does not begin until after the Park Road/Manorgate Road junction, a few yards ahead of the tram. This view, taken around 1907, looks east towards the hill from a point just beyond the London Road railway bridge. On the left is the signboard of William Rogers, piano tuner, repairer and dealer, at no. 185. Next door, at 187, is the Cigar Box, a tobacco shop run by Ernest Doo. Then comes the substantial, double-fronted shop of Denny & Sons, well-known local dairymen. The shopping terrace beyond includes a grocer, a carver and gilder, and an outfitter. On the right, just beyond the shop and cyclist, is the Black Horse pub, with a prominent signpost set on the kerbside. Beyond the pub is Manorgate Road then, clearly visible on the corner, the handsome new branch of the London and South Western Bank at 2 Kingston Hill. This was subsequently taken over by Barclays, who still occupy the premises today. The Black Horse was later demolished and rebuilt several yards back from the road.

Kingston Hill. *(Publ: A.S. No 364. Postally unused.)*

The summit of Kingston Hill, looking towards Kingston. The only clue to this location is the distinctive tower, visible over the hedge on the left. This was part of the Metropolitan Children's Convalescent Home in Gloucester Road (re-named Galsworthy Road in 1967) which was opened by the Prince and Princess of Wales in 1875. Later the building was bought by the National Society for the Protection of Young Girls and was opened by Princess Louise in 1892 as a home "to protect young girls between the ages of 11 and 15 years, whether orphans or otherwise, who may be in danger of leading depraved lives and to feed, clothe, educate and train them for domestic service and laundry work." Later the premises became a Dr. Barnardo's orphanage. The building was demolished in 1969 to make way for Blenheim Gardens. The tall chimney to the right of the tower belonged to Kingston Workhouse.

Kingston Vale — Robin Hood Hotel. *(Publ: The Collectors' Publ. Co. Postally used 1910.)*

Kingston Vale runs south-west to Kingston Hill from the Robin Hood Roundabout on the A3. The Robin Hood Hotel was built in 1870 to replace a far older inn with the same name. It was popular with travellers and trippers because it offered good bedrooms, attractive tea gardens and stabling for 30 horses. It also had the advantage of being the only fully licensed pub that the Duke of Cambridge would allow on his extensive estates in the area. The passing car represents an early warning that the Robin Hood's long career as a coaching inn was entering its final phase when this picture was taken. Today the stabling has given way to car parking, but the main Victorian frontage remains unaltered except that the main entrance is now through what was the centre of the bay window. For many years it was a popular Berni Inn, which has now become a Beefeater house.

Kingston Vale, Kingston Road.   *(Publ: The Collectors' Publ. Co. "Mercury" series. Postally used 1907.)*

The only surviving feature of this scene is the walling on the left. The road has evolved into the roaringly busy A3 and the country hedges have gone to make way for road widening, houses and a Smiths Industries factory — now acquired by Kingston Polytechnic. However part of the pasture to the right of the fingerpost survives as the Richardson Evans Memorial Playing Fields.

The shot is taken just north of the famous Robin Hood Roundabout, near the Robin Hood gate into Richmond Park. In the far distance in the modern picture can be seen the latest large building complex — Asda Supermarket — which has necessitated considerable road reconstruction for easy access.

Landing Stage and River Terrace, Nuthall's Ltd. K-on-T.   *(Publ: Morland Studio, K-o-T. Postally unused.)*

The hub of smart social life in Edwardian Kingston was Nuthall's, an old-established catering firm who, in 1902, opened ornate new premises at 3/5 Thames Street. It had beautiful gardens stretching down to the river and made a speciality of providing for punting parties. Here a group prepares to disembark at Nuthall's landing stage, perhaps for afternoon tea, or cool drinks in the garden. On the river are two laden timber barges, probably from Gridley Miskin, whose timberyards were on the waterfront at Bucklands Wharf, just downstream from Kingston Bridge.   For all its elegance, Nuthall's never recovered from World War I and the depression that followed. In 1933 it closed and the building was converted into a branch of British Home Stores.   Now it is occupied by Millets. Meanwhile the former gardens are covered by the Gazebo pub and part of the public Riverside Walk. However the landing steps and the two distinctive summerhouses (only one of which is visible here) still survive.

Afternoon Tea, Rosebery Hall, Nuthall's Ltd. K-o-T.   *(Publ: Morland Studio, K-o-T. Postally unused.)*

The Rosebery Hall was named in honour of the 5th Earl of Rosebery who attended a lavish banquet here on October 17th 1901 — the day he became High Steward of Kingston. The rest of Nuthall's palatial new premises

were not completed until the following March. The Rosebery Hall was on the ground floor, behind Nuthall's elegant tea, coffee and provisions shops. Two sets of glass doors, seen on the right, (above) led to the riverside gardens.

The building also contained the King's Hall, the Knights Room and several private banqueting suites, plus an acre of wine cellars, extensive kitchens and bakery and confectionery departments. In the Rosebery Hall, Luncheon could be had daily for 2/6d (twelve and a half pence). There were also nightly dinner dances for 4/- (twenty pence) per guest and tea dances on Saturday afternoons with Cyril J. Gardener's Band in attendance.

Nuthall's as it looked when opened in 1902.

The Bridge, Kingston-on-Thames.   (*Publ: Valentine's Series No. 07479. Postally unused.*)

Kingston's handsome stone bridge was opened by the Duchess of Clarence (later Queen Adelaide, consort of William IV) in 1828, and replaced a narrow, timber structure dating from the 12th century. In 1914 it was widened on the upstream side. This photograph, taken from the Middlesex side of the river in the early years of this century, shows the importance of the Thames as a local leisure and social amenity. Small boys are happily engaged in paddling and fishing in its waters. Young bloods display their punting skills. Family groups take to the oars. Those not on the water stand on the river bank, or on the bridge, enjoying their role as spectators. Through the central arch of the bridge is a distant view of Turk's, which still survives on the site as the oldest family boat firm on the Thames. A walk along the Middlesex towpath to-day gives a view of a much-changed Kingston, dominated by the John Lewis complex to the right of the bridge and the two giant chimneys of the now-defunct Power Station.

Kingston. View from the Bridge. *(Publ: Frith's Series. Postally used 1905.)*

This card captures some of the atmosphere of the days when the Thames was the exhuberant social hub of Kingston, and families owned rowing boats much as they do cars to-day. The local clergy frequently lamented that the biggest obstacle to their work was not the demon drink, as in other towns, but the river. In this typical scene crowds throng the Barge Walk on the Middlesex Bank. Over on the Kingston side can be seen the Sun Hotel landing stage. Then the riverside premises of Burgoine's, who built many important Thames craft in Victorian and Edwardian days, some of them for the Royal family. The tall chimney denotes the Eagle Brewery, and beyond that is the busy commercial Town End Wharf. Unlike now, there was no riverside walk on this stretch of the Thames until Queen's Promenade, whose curving line is just visible in the far distance, beyond Town End Wharf. As the modern picture shows, the river bank is now more popular than the river itself, which is often empty of traffic.

High Street and River, Kingston.　　　　　　　　　*(Publ: A.S. Series No. 256. Postally used 1904.)*

High Street — picturesquely known as West-by-Thames until late Victorian times — was for centuries the industrial and commercial hub of Kingston. In 1990 archaeologists discovered the remains of a medieval industrial complex, specialising in pottery production and iron working, with samples of pottery dating from about 1250 to 1400. By the 19th century the street included several malthouses, the Eagle Brewery, a gin distillery, dyeworks, boatbuilders, a few shops and Harris's Iron Foundry. Several items of Harris's work survive in the town in the form of railings and bollards. On the left is the busy Town End Wharf, used for the receipt and despatch of various cargo. To-day High Street is still recovering from years of planning blight caused by Kingston Council's scheme to route the town centre relief road along the river frontage — a scheme that never happened. Town End Wharf now provides short-term moorings for private pleasure craft, and an office block stands on the site of Harris's Foundry.

Portsmouth Road, Kingston. *(Publ: A.S. Series No. 365. Postally used 1905.)*

Every building but one on this picture has disappeared. But it's still possible to recognise the spot because that little grass island still survives, though minus its mature trees and the sturdy stone drinking trough, here providing welcome refreshment for a passing horse. Just visible on the left is the riverside Queen's Promenade. The domed building just beyond the island is The Anglers, built in 1901 to replace a far older pub of the same name. To the right of The Anglers can be seen a small part of the 17th century building that is now the Hermes Hotel.

Today Queen's Promenade and its trees and railings still survive. But The Anglers was demolished in 1959 and replaced by a block of flats, and the fine old houses on the right have given way to a garage and filling station. Also gone is the drinking trough and the working horses who used it. Cars dominate the scene now. Indeed, it could be said that the petrol station on the right is the modern counterpart of the trough!

St Raphael R.C. Church, Kingston.   *(Publ: British Mirror Series, No.117/16. Postally used 1907.)*

There is a strange but true story attached to this church, which overlooks the river in Portsmouth Road between Surbiton Road and Riverside Close. It was built by Alexander Raphael, who fell gravely ill in the 1840's. As he lay dying he vowed to the Virgin Mary that if she would intercede for his recovery he would build a church. He did recover, and the result was the beautiful little church which he had constructed at a time when there was no other RC church in Kingston. It was completed in 1848 and was due to open that year. However, Mr Raphael had a dream which foretold his death soon after the church's consecration. He therefore delayed the ceremony, cancelling several appointments with Bishop Nicholas Wiseman, head of what was then known as the London District. Then, in 1850, Mr Raphael went away, forgetting to cancel yet another date for the consecration. The Bishop arrived, got the key from the butler, and went ahead with the service. Mr Raphael died soon afterwards, just as his dream foretold. Now his remains lie beneath the High Altar of the church he never used.

The Union Hotel, Surbiton Park Terrace, Kingston-on-Thames.   *(photo: Russell, Surbiton. Postally unused.)*
The Union Hotel was one of the most elegant pub buildings ever seen in Kingston when it was constructed in 1854. Fricker's Eagle Brewery planned it to be a fitting port of call for respectable businessmen travelling between Kingston and the new and fashionable district of Surbiton.   There were many of them, for the so-called Kingston Station was located at Surbiton then. There was no station in Kingston itself until 1863.   The name Fricker disappeared from the handsome frontage in 1903, when Fricker's Brewery was bought by Hodgson's. The Union closed in 1978 when Courage, successors to Hodgson's, sold it for use as offices.   Fortunately Fricker's elegant frontage has survived virtually intact, and is at present occupied by Lundby of Sweden Ltd.
Surbiton Park Terrace forms part of Surbiton Road, which runs south east from the river to Surbiton Hill.

Surbiton Park Terrace, Kingston.   *(Publ: R.S. & Co. 136 Old Street, London E.C. No. 23. Postally used 1907.)*
Surbiton Park Terrace was built on the east side of Surbiton Road in 1851 as a smart shopping parade to serve the elegant residential roads that quickly took shape after the death of Alexander Raphael in 1850. Much of the wooded parkland surrounding his mansion, Surbiton Hall, was bought by a developer named William Woods and transformed into Surbiton Crescent and the Anglesea, Palace and Uxbridge Roads. When this picture was taken of the south end, looking towards Kingston, the terrace had a wide variety of shops including a plumber, tailor, piano showroom, chemist, draper, staymaker, grocer, fruiterer, picture frame maker, shoemaker and dressmaker. The terrace survives largely unchanged save for the removal of the interesting window-detailing on all but one of the shops, and the addition of some unsympathetic modern shopfronts and fascias. The trees and the wrought-iron lamp posts of old are also a sad loss.

SURBITON

Portsmouth Road, Surbiton.
(Publ: Bull & Son, Surbiton. No. 97882. Postally unused.)

This picture was taken in 1907. Behind the trees on the right are large houses designed in the mid-19th century for what their developers described as "the nobility and gentry." On the left are the railings separating the road from Queen's Promenade and the river. Cyclists and a two-horse van are the only traffic and a dog ambles peacefully down the central highway.

Today all but two of the mansions have been replaced by flats and no dog would survive long in the road. However, apart from the demise of the elegant street lamp, the left side of the road remains the same, the railings, trees and Queen's Promenade still intact.

Raven's Ait Ferry, Surbiton. *(Publ: Bull & Son, Surbiton. Postally used 1912).*

Their graceful summer clothes, plus the picnic basket suggests that these ladies have been — or are going — to one of the garden parties or other smart events organised by Kingston Rowing Club after it established its headquarters on Raven's Ait in 1858.   The ferry to the island still operates, but with a trim, canopied boat launched early in 1992. Ravens Ait, partly visible on the far left of both pictures, was known for centuries as Ravens Arse! It was used for growing osiers, a type of willow needed for the hand-made baskets which were a local industry in Kingston until the 19th century.   The 1.5 -acre island was bought by Kingston Council for £1.4 million in 1989 and is now used for conferences and social functions, and as a water sports centre run by the National School of Sailing and the British Canoe Union. Note how Queen's Promenade has been divided into upper and lower paths in modern times.

The Globe & Portsmouth Road, Surbiton. *(Publ: anon. Postally unused.)*

The handsome Globe public house first appears in local street directories in 1864. It was built for Hodgson's Kingston Brewery, and dominated the junction of Portsmouth Road and Brighton Road until it closed in September 1962. When this picture was taken, around 1910, The Globe was tenanted by Frederick Sleigh, whose name is over the main entrance. The two towers rising up behind are part of the Chelsea Water Co's works, built alongside the turnpike road to Portsmouth in 1852. The twin battlemented towers, just visible above the tramcar, belonged to the Lambeth Water Co. whose works were completed on an adjoining site in 1851. By the time of this photograph, both works were being run by the Metropolitan Water Board. Trams were introduced to Kingston in 1906. This one is on its route to Kingston from the terminus at Windows Bridge (often known as Winters Bridge) Thames Ditton. In 1973 The Globe was converted into showrooms for John Ashley Motors, who still occupy the premises to-day.

Brighton Road, Surbiton. *(Publ: Rotary Photo. London E.C. Postally used 1911.)*

The years 1904 and 1905 greatly enhanced Brighton Road as a shopping centre. Brighton Terrace, a row of houses on the north side between Cottage Grove and Victoria Grove were converted into shops (visible in the middle distance, on the left) and the flamboyantly handsome Electric Parade was completed, with its "Dutch Renaissance" gables and clock tower. The clock was blown out of the tower by a bomb during World War II, and has never been replaced. Otherwise Electric Parade remains unscathed. The road in the right foreground is Balaclava Road, with Surbiton Baptist Church partially visible. Opposite, on the left of the picture, is Maple Road with the Black Lion pub on the corner. Why the name Electric Parade? Probably because 1904 saw the official opening of the Surbiton Electricity Works, and that same year electric cables were extended to Brighton Road. The sense of wonder at the new power did not last. Within five years the name Electric Parade had been dropped and today it refers only to an alley running behind the shops.

Brighton Road, Surbiton.   *(Publ: M.J.R. B. — M.J.Ridley, Bournemouth. 7142. Postally unused.)*
This view looks west from the junction with Victoria Avenue on the left and Victoria Road on the right. On the corner of Victoria Road is the curving shop frontage of Lane & Son. John Lane was among the first traders in Victoria Road, his name appearing in a trade directory of 1845 as a stonemason. Later his business was in furnishings, ironmongery etc. and by the 1860's he had another shop in Surbiton Park Terrace. It is now occupied by Sharps Bedrooms.   On the left, from the corner of Victoria Avenue, is The Broadway, a row of six shops built in 1900 and 1901. Adjoining The Broadway is Electric Parade (built in stages from 1902 to 1905) whose high gables and clock tower (just visible above the tram) are still features of the road today. There is no date on the card, but trams did not appear until 1906.

John R. Gillett Advertising Postcard. *(Publ: Russell, Surbiton. Postally used 1907.)*

Joseph Ryland sent one of his sales postcards to Mrs W. Mudie of Brighton Road in 1906. The following year his rival John R. Gillett, whose shop was on the opposite side of Victoria Road at no. 54, sent this similar card to Mrs Mudie at the same address. The Gillett shop site now forms part of the Sainsbury/YMCA complex, completed in 1980. It is interesting to note that there are still a few shops in Victoria Road that have been trading for over 50 years, notably F.P.Turner & Sons, Jewellers; Victoria Wine Co. Ltd., Wine & Spirit Merchants; Bull & Son, Stationers, who once had their own printing presses at 20 Victoria Street, and published many local postcards. And Sainsburys, who were originally at 2 and 3, in the premises now occupied by Lewis Meeson.

J.E.Ryland Advertising Postcard. *(Postally used July 1906.)*

The enterprising Joseph Ryland had this postcard specially printed and posted to customers to advertise his summer sale in July 1906. "The production of this card entitles the bearer to a further reduction of one penny in the shilling," says the message on the back. Mr Ryland describes himself as a general and fancy draper, and gives his address as Victoria House, Surbiton. In fact it was 27 Victoria Road, and his trim premises on the St. Andrew's Road corner have now been replaced by a modern building, which for the last few years was occupied by a clothes shop — Seconds Out. This closed in 1992.

Victoria Road, Surbiton. *(Publ: Bull & Son, Surbiton. No.113831. Postally unused.)*

The most interesting features of this picture are the three trams with their covered tops. This was the design used to launch the local tramway system in March 1906. However, these vehicles graced the streets for only a year before being replaced by a cheaper, open-topped model which remained in use until trams were superseded by trolley buses in 1931. This view looks towards the junction of St. Mark's Hill with St. James Road and Claremont Road. Prominent on the left is Madame Bonnert's fashion salon at No. 7, the entrance guarded by expensive wrought-iron balustrading. Madame Bonnert advertised herself in discreet advertisements as a "court dressmaker" specialising in "dinner and reception gowns, wedding trousseaux and colonial outfits." She probably regretted having to share the premises with the Stratton Gentry Coal Office, whose image was at odds with hers! Next door at number 8, shielded by a striped blind, is H.Packham & Sons, famous over many decades as bakers, confectioners and caterers. Today the attractive wrought-iron terracing has disappeared from the upper frontages on the left.

Surbiton Railway Station. *(Publ: A.S. Series No. 96. Postally used 1909.)*

In 1837, when Queen Victoria was crowned, Surbiton had a population of 200. By 1852 it had risen to 2,800; and by 1887, the Queen's Golden Jubilee, it had increased to 10,500. Surbiton's transformation from ancient hamlet to fashionable suburb was the result of a scheme, conceived in 1830, to make a railway from London to Southampton. The Southampton and London Railway Company was formed in 1832, sanctioned by an Act of Parliament in 1834 and the first stretch of the line, from Nine Elms to Woking, was opened in 1838. It was to have skirted Kingston town. Instead, because of opposition, it was run through a deep cutting at Surbiton, with a tiny station on the south side of the line near the Ewell Road bridge. In 1840 Thomas Pooley, the original developer of Surbiton, induced the railway company to move the station to its present position where many improvements were made in 1887. The Southampton Hotel (right) was demolished in 1960, replaced by a modern pub — itself razed in 1988 for offices.

Claremont Road Garden, Surbiton.   *(Publ: anon. Postally used 1927)*

Claremont Road, known originally as Railway Road, was laid out by Thomas Pooley in 1840 to provide a convenient route between the newly-opened station at Surbiton and Kingston. At the same time he created Claremont Crescent, now known simply as The Crescent, and moved into the first completed house there. The semicircular space between the two roads later became Claremont Gardens, a pretty oasis designed for the exclusive use of residents. However, the gardens eventually became derelict. They were rescued by Surbiton Council who bought the site in 1926, restored the landscaping and opened it as a public park. "There is a picturesque waterfall with a winding brook leading to a large pond, where small children may sail their boats in perfect safety", noted the Surbiton Guide of 1957. Alas, the waterfall has since disappeared, and the pond is an empty pit. The thatched shelter, amazingly, is still there; but, like so many public places today, it has been disfigured by graffiti pests.

Adelaide Road, Surbiton. *(Publ: anon. No. 15160. Perf. edge. Postally unused.)*

Adelaide Road leads off St.Mark's Hill, and runs parallel with Claremont Road. Known originally as Church Road, it was one of the first roads to be laid out after Thomas Pooley bought the Maple Farm estate in 1838 and, inspired by the newly-opened station, began creating what he envisaged as the new town of Kingston-on-Railway. However, by 1842 he was in financial straits and his new town, re-named Surbiton, was taken over by Coutts Bank, who dismantled many of his buildings and changed his place names. Pooley had displayed his Royalist loyalties by creating three terraces named after Victoria, Albert and Adelaide. Victoria terrace survives as the first eight buildings on the north side of Victoria Road. The whole of Albert Terrace, and all but two of Adelaide Terrace's fourteen houses, were destroyed by Pooley's successors. But they retained the name of Adelaide, consort of William IV, by using it to re-label Church Road.

Maple Road, Surbiton.   *(Publ: A.S. Series No. 74. Postally used 1908.)*

Maple Road began life as Terry's Lane, a narrow muddy track that was the only thoroughfare between Ewell Road and Brighton Road. It ran across the fields of Maple Farm, which was owned by gentleman farmer Christopher Terry. After Mr Terry's death in 1838 most of his 150-acre estate was bought by Thomas Pooley, a Kingston maltster who conceived the idea of creating an elegant new town around the brand-new station at Surbiton. When Mr Pooley faced ruin in 1844 he had only developed the southern end of Maple Road, which he named Hampton Grove. The rest was transformed in 1856, from a muddy country lane to the handsome road we know to-day, when the water companies were building their new filter beds alongside the Thames at Seething Wells. Their giant mains had to be brought along the lane, and the Surbiton Commissioners insisted that while so doing, the water companies should make it up and widen it. So the ratepayers of Surbiton got the road for nothing.

The Waggon & Horses, Surbiton Hill. *(Photographed circa 1885)*

The Waggon & Horses was established in Stuart times and became a famous house of call for packmen and carriers. It occupied a desolate spot on the edge of what was then the wild expanse of Surbiton Common. The public gallows stood close by until their transfer to the Kingston Hill area (reputedly in the 18th century), and immediately to the south of the pub was the public pound and gate, where stray animals were impounded, and not released until a fixed fee had been paid. The gate was to prevent livestock straying on to the common. Yet the pub's position was its greatest asset; for laden waggons needed an extra horse to get them up Surbiton Hill, and a horse was always kept in readyness at the pub for this purpose. Hence the name Waggon & Horses. The original Waggon & Horses, pictured here shortly before its demolition, was constructed largely of overlapping timbers. It was re-built in 1888 by Young's Brewery, when Surbiton had evolved from a lonely hamlet to a fashionable suburb.

Cranes Park Road, Surbiton. *(Publ: A.S. Series No. 4515. Postally used 1923)*

The Cranes was originally a 52-acre estate owned by the prominent local Jemmett family (the Jemmetts were virtually hereditary Town Clerks of Kingston, three succeeding generations holding the office for about a century from 1747). It was auctioned off in May 1885 as *" unrivalled sites for the erection of first-class residences....situate in the heart of this favourite neighbourhood, only a few minutes walk from the river Thames and Surbiton Station as well as a proposed station on the intended extension of the Metropolitan District Railway from Fulham to Surbiton."* The residences materialised after Cranes Park and Cranes Park Avenue had been cut through the estate, leaving the mansion in a triangle formed by these two new roads and Villiers Avenue. By 1914 the house, too, had disappeared to make way for Cranes Park Crescent and Cranes Park Road. The latter, pictured here from the Villiers Avenue end around 1920, still retains much of its character. The whole area has always been the very acme of prosperous respectability.

War Memorial, Surbiton.   *(Publ: A.S. No. 4664. Postally unused.)*

Surbiton's memorial to the dead of World War 1 occupied an attractive, open plot in Ewell Road when it was first put up (the houses on the right are the backs of Shalston Villas).

Now it is hemmed in by the Fire Brigade station on the right and Surbiton Library Hall to the left, with the Citizen's Advice Bureau behind. Remembrance Day services continue to be held here in the presence of local councillors and representatives of local organisations, and many of the public, although the traffic is no longer stopped on the Ewell Road at the eleventh hour.

Ewell Road, Surbiton. *(Publ: A.S. Series No. 85. Postally unused.)*

The tramlines have long since gone and there is now a proliferation of modern road signs and street furniture. Otherwise this view of the northern end of Ewell Road, looking towards Kingston, survives remarkably unchanged. Some of the distinctive houses on the right are said to have been specially designed to display the variety of bricks and tiles produced by Robert Brown's brickfields that once flourished on a site off Ewell Road, and which are remembered in the name of Brown's Road. The church spire belongs to Surbiton Methodist Church. This was dedicated in 1882, and replaced the temporary iron church opened on the site in 1876. No local materials were used. The building, designed in early gothic style by London architect Charles Bell, incorporates red Leicester bricks with Bath stone dressings!

Ewell Road, Surbiton. *(Publ: Bull & Son, Surbiton. No. 102526. Postally unused.)*

This picture is taken from near the same spot as that on page 58, but looking the other way — down the hill towards Tolworth. Just beyond the young trees on the left is a tall sign proclaiming *The Plough*. This old pub, known to have existed in pre-Victorian times, is still there to-day, though its stabling is now a car showroom! In pre-railway times it stood alone, with open fields on either side, and was an important place of call for travellers. For, rutted and rural though it was, Ewell Road had been a vital thoroughfare for centuries. Until 1871 it was a turnpike road which meant that anyone travelling in a vehicle had to pay to pass through the toll gates set up at intervals along the route. There was one such gate on Surbiton Hill, near the Waggon & Horses, and another — the Tolworth Gate — close to what is now Broomfield Road. Local residents were delighted to be rid of the tolls — until they found their rates would have to replace tolls in maintaining the road! The shops on the right were built originally as private houses.

Lane by Berrylands Farm, Surbiton. *(Publ: A.S. No. 417. Postally unused.)*

This postcard is labelled simply "Lane by Berrylands Farm, Surbiton." However, its original owner testified that the picture was taken in June 1913 and the lane later became Manor Drive. The farm buildings stood on a site now bounded by Berrylands, Manor Drive, Kings Drive and Pine Walk, and the view to the east was of open fields all the way to Malden. There was much regret locally when the farm was sold for housing development in 1930. "Goodbye, dear old Berrylands," mourned the *Surrey Comet* of July 1930. "An ever-advancing civilisation (?) is spreading its bricks and mortar over the hay-grass of your fragrant meadows, and it is certain that, sooner rather than later, the very spot where once you triumphed is forgot." The modern picture of Manor Drive, taken from the Courtlands Road end, doesn't of course bear any resemblance to the original lane — except that there appears to be a wide variety of trees in both eras.

Surbiton Lagoon.
(Publ: anon. Postally used 1934.)

The growing popularity of open-air bathing led Surbiton Urban District Council to build Surbiton Lagoon in 1933 on a two-and-a-half acre site in Raeburn Avenue. It consisted of a swimming bath and toddlers' pool plus three hard tennis courts, a sandpit and landscaped areas. The bath was a showpiece of its time, measuring 165 feet by 90 feet, and containing half a million gallons of water which were cleansed every six hours by the Lagoon's own filter plant. This picture was taken soon after the official opening in 1934. On the right is the stepped terrace, which could hold a thousand spectators at swimming galas and water polo matches.

Surbiton Lagoon was closed "for repairs" in 1979. It has never re-opened and the future of the site has been a controversial topic ever since. In fact, as today's picture shows it has reverted to something like what it was before the lagoon was built — a reversal of the usual process!

The Avenue, known at first as Berrylands, was laid out in the 1840's, but it took several years to complete it with pleasant, individually designed houses on its north, east and west sides. As can be seen in the modern photograph it looks much the same to-day. This road lies in the heart of the Berrylands district which derives its name from Berrylands Farm and Berry Lodge Farm. These adjoined one another for centuries to the north-east of what is now Berrylands Road.

In the 18th century Berrylands Farm had 130 acres and Berry Lodge 219, and they lay

The Avenue, Surbiton Hill.
(Publ: A.S. Series No. 86. Postally unused.)

isolated amid the great tracts of Surbiton Common, that stretched all the way to Hook and Chessington. An advertisement of 1913 describes Berrylands Farm as having 317 acres. Presumably some of this was land acquired from Berry Lodge Farm, which was the first to disappear. Berrylands Farm's homestead was destroyed for road building in 1882, but the farm and several outbuildings survived for the next half-century, supplying much of Kingston and Surbiton with milk from its dairies at 129 Richmond Road and 16 Brighton Road. Now all the fields of both farms are covered by residential roads.

Manor House Convent and School, Surbiton Hill.   *(Publ: anon. Postally unused.)*

Manor House Convent and School stood at 9 to 13 The Avenue until it was demolished by developers amid a storm of protest in 1983. Though it had been altered and extended since early Victorian times, the building was said to have an inner core dating back 200 years. The School was established in Clifton, Bristol's famous Georgian suburb, in 1881. It was acquired by the French order of nuns, the Dames de la Mere de Dieu, and moved to Surbiton when its premises, Manilla Hall, had to be demolished. The school had such a fine reputation that its boarding pupils made the move from Clifton to Surbiton as well. The billiard room at Manor House was converted into a chapel which was linked to the Roman Catholic church of St. Raphael on the Kingston riverside. The school could accommodate up to 150 pupils, and enrolled all nationalities and religions. To-day the site is covered by Hever House, a modern apartment block, and all that is left of Manor House is its gateposts, shown in the picture below.

The Prince of Wales/The New Prince   *(From an old photograph — pre-1907)*

The origins of The Prince of Wales at Ewell Road, Surbiton are lost in the mists of time. But it's known to have been refreshing travellers for at least 150 years, first as a beerhouse, and then as a fully-fledged pub. Customers inside are crowding round the windows to watch the photographer at work, and the carefully posed people on the forecourt all seem — with the exception of the man in shirtsleeves — to be wearing their Sunday best. The smart little carriage may belong to a customer, or it may be one of those hired out by the carriage proprietor, B. Forder, whose sign is displayed on the left side, just above the ground floor bay window. The old cottage adjoining the pub on the right bears the prominent sign of Harry Rushworth, the local plumber, decorator and carpenter. The Prince of Wales continued in Charrington's ownership until 1991. Then it was bought by Mr Harry McArdle, previously mine host at The Brittania in Alpha Road, Surbiton. He completely re-modelled the interior and re-opened it in March 1992 as a free house. He also re-named it The New Prince to mark the start of a new chapter in its long history.

Oak Hill, Surbiton.
(Publ: anon. Postally used 1908.)

Surbiton in the old days was not as grand as many people imagine. That oft-repeated label "Queen of the Suburbs" was, in fact, merely an advertising cliche used by agents to describe not only Surbiton but many other new developments in the great Victorian post-railway building boom. However, there was a touch of grandeur about the Oakhill area. It was developed in the 1850's by William Clerk, who built such imposing houses, set in such spacious grounds, that his taste outran his capital and he went bankrupt in 1855. Though most of his houses have been demolished or converted, and their grounds developed, Oakhill and the other roads on Clerk's estate still retain something of their original character because so many trees have been retained.

Lovelace Gardens, Surbiton. *(Publ: A.S. Series No. 84. Postally unused.)*

Lovelace Gardens, like neighbouring Lovelace Road, was created in 1882, following the sale of the beautiful Southborough Estate for housing. It was named after the 1st Earl of Lovelace, who owned 15,000 acres in Surrey, including much of Surbiton and Hook, and was Lord Lieutenant of the County for 53 years, only resigning just before his death in 1893. Today he is better known for having married Ada, the only legitimate child of the poet, Lord Byron.

Many of the fine old houses have since been demolished to make way for blocks of flats, and the modern street lamps have none of the charm of their predecessors.

Ditton Road, Surbiton. *(Publ: A.S. No. 93. Postally used 1912.)*

The Ordnance Survey of 1865 shows Ditton Road bounded by fields on both sides, no buildings at all until Hill Farm, which stood roughly where Ditton Road becomes Ditton Hill, just past the junction with Langley Avenue *(seen here on the right)*. By the 1890's Ditton Road had houses on both sides, several of them "gentlemen's residences" set in leafy gardens. This view is looking towards Long Ditton. The gateway and entrance lodge on the left belong to a handsome house, set in six acres, that was built in 1881 as *The Mount*, later re-named *Haulkerton*. In 1910 it was acquired for Shrewsbury House School, founded by the Rev. Henry Wilson in 1865 as a "preparatory tutorial establishment for boys". It began in *Claremont Villas*, moving in 1880 to *Shrewsbury House* at 11 Claremont Crescent (from which it took its name). Pupils increased, and in 1893 it moved to a large house in Maple Road, opposite Surbiton Assembly Rooms. Here it stayed until the move to Ditton Road where it flourishes to this day.

Langley Avenue, Surbiton. *(Publ: A.S. Series No. 266. Postally unused.)*

This photograph was probably taken in 1904. Langley Avenue was one of the roads laid out in 1882 after most of the park and farmland surrounding Southborough Lodge was sold off for housing. It is named after Thomas Langley, who had Southborough Lodge designed for him by the famous architect John Nash in 1808. This fine house still survives in Ashcombe Avenue.

Note the lady on the left, about to brave public opinion by mounting her bicycle. So many women were taking to the saddle that in 1904 the *Surrey Comet* published an editorial deploring the practice and censuring the divided skirts worn by many female cyclists!

TOLWORTH AND HOOK

Tolworth Tower

Until the early 1880's, Tolworth was known as Talworth, and was a hamlet in the parish of Long Ditton consisting almost entirely of farms and common land. Its population in 1871 was only 464, and by the dawn of the 20th century had still not reached a thousand. It increased steadily after that as farmland gave way to housing, and so attracted new families. But what really revolutionised Tolworth was the opening of Kingston By-pass in 1927. It resulted in an economic and environmental upheaval epitomised by the building of Tolworth Tower, seen here soon after its completion in 1963. (Previously, part of the site had been occupied by an Odeon cinema, opened in 1934 and closed in 1959).

Tolworth Tower made national headlines as the tallest and largest office development in the Home Counties at that time, its 22 storeys soaring 235 feet above the By-pass. Its first ground-floor tenant was Fine Fare, which opened what was then the largest supermarket in Europe. Today it is occupied by a Marks and Spencer foodstore.

Tolworth Fountain, Surbiton. *(Publ: A.S. No. 263. Postally unused.)*

For centuries there was a horse pond in the Ewell Road at Tolworth. But after Tolworth had officially become part of Surbiton a dispute arose: did the pond belong to Lord Egmont, who owned hundreds of acres in and around Tolworth, or to Surbiton Local Board? Eventually the Board won and gave the pond to a prominent local contractor, Stephen Kavanagh, who needed it for rubbish disposal. In exchange, Mr Kavanagh gave the Board two plots of land and a handsome drinking fountain, surmounted by a thousand candle power lamp. The fountain — designed for use by humans, sheep, cattle, horses and dogs — was inaugurated with great ceremony in 1903. In 1936 it was removed for road improvements. Its remains were unearthed near Kingston By-pass in 1973. The building on the left, little changed today is on the corner of Beaconsfield Road, and at the time was occupied by a wine & spirit merchant named Wirth. He was much pilloried by locals during World War I because of his German ancestry.

By the Fountain, Tolworth.   *(Publ: A.S. Series No. 2496. Postally used 1928.)*

This view of the fountain is dominated by St. Matthew's Church which was built in 1875 just inside the Surbiton boundary, on the corner of St Matthew's Avenue and Kingsdowne Road. Ewell Road sweeps round out of sight towards Kingston, and Kingsdowne Road is viewed looking up to meet Upper Brighton Road. The church was designed by the Surbiton architect, Charles Luck, and is noted for its graceful spire, which rises 170 feet.

Today Hinton & Wild occupy the building on the corner of Ditton Road, which until 1989 was Barclays Bank, opposite where the old Police Station used to be.

Church of Our lady Immaculate, Tolworth. Surrey. *(Publ: Anon. Postally unused)*

This church was born in the early 1930's as the "daughter" of St. Raphael's Roman Catholic Church in Portsmouth Road, and continued as such until it achieved parochial status and its own purpose-built church some 25 years later. During that time the congregation worshipped in the tiny chapel visible here on the right, sandwiched between the church and the neighbouring houses. The foundation stone of the new building was laid in April 1956 and this postcard was probably produced to mark its completion the following year.

The church remains the same. But the trolley bus wires disapppeared in 1962, when motor buses were introduced. The road sweeping round to the far right is the continuation of the original Ewell Road, which now meets the A3 to London.

Ewell Road Bridge, Tolworth.   *(Publ: A.S. Series No. 540. Postally unused — circa 1900.)*

This tranquil country scene disappeared after the construction of Kingston By-pass. In 1938 the Ewell Road, Tolworth was widened and partially straightened between the By-pass and the bridge. However, a small section of the old road just south of the By-pass still survives (*Old Kingston Road*). So does a portion of this bridge over the Hogsmill River, which marked the municipal boundary between Surbiton and Epsom. The signpost in the middle distance *(above)* indicates the junction with Old Malden Lane, now called Worcester Park Road. As the horse and cart and bicycle gave way to the motor car, the junction altered to the point where to-day, recently completed work has afforded a new layout of slip roads funnelling traffic on to and off the main road through the inevitable phasing of the traffic lights.

Tolworth Broadway.   *(Publ: Lees, The Card Shop, 104, Broadway, Tolworth. No. LD 4. Postally unused.)*
Tolworth Broadway was carved through the pastures of Tolworth Lodge Farm after the farm had been sold for development in 1931. It was a pedestrian's paradise—note the unusually wide pavement on the left and the grassy verges on the right, where shop-building is still in progress. But it was a good life for motorists, too, with unrestricted parking on both sides of the concrete block road which looks novel to modern eyes but was a feature of that period. In the distance, on the right, can be seen the Church of Our Lady Immaculate. It stands on the corner opposite the service station where Tolworth Lodge farmhouse once stood.

Now Tolworth Broadway is a dual carriageway, bisected by an iron barrier to keep pedestrians at bay. The modern photograph was taken from the edge of the large roundabout which now spans the top of the A3 underpass.

The Broadway, Tolworth.   *(Publ: Frith's Series TTH.13F. Postally unused.)*

A slightly later view of Tolworth Broadway, its east side now complete and in business. Nowadays the dual carriageway can be crossed only by a pedestrian underpass, or at traffic lights adjacent to Tolworth Tower.

Tolworth Rise *(Oak Cabin Series Postally unused.)*

On October 28th, 1927 the Prime Minister, Stanley Baldwin, opened "the eight and a half miles of new arterial road which has come to be known as the Kingston By-Pass Road." Running from Kingston Vale to Hinchley Wood, it was the first by-pass in Britain, and set in train a huge wave of residential development on what had previously been rich farmlands. Within three years, six and a half miles of new streets had been laid out and nearly 2,000 houses and 57 shops built. This view of the newly-completed Tolworth Rise typifies residential development at that time. The "Tudorbethan" style was much in vogue, as illustrated by the shops on the left and the timbering and steep gables of the houses on the right.   The photographs were taken from a position near Elmbridge Avenue which is nowadays reached by a slip road running parallel to this busy A3.

Hook Road, (Showing Recreation Ground) Surbiton. *(Publ: T.Seymour, Hook Rd., Surbiton. Postally used 1917.)*
King Edward Recreation Ground was opened in 1901 on what had been six acres of wheatfields. It was named in honour of the new King Edward VII, and was a major addition to what was still the small rural village of Hook. In 1964 the road was made into a dual carriageway. As a result, the houses on the right lost part of their front gardens while pedestrians had to forego the pretty sunken footpath which ran alongside the recreation ground, shielded from the road by a hedge.

Just out of sight on the left hand corner is St. Paul's Hall. Behind the recreation ground, down the lane, is the home of Kingston Rugby Football Club, which, founded in 1887, is one of the oldest Clubs in Surrey.

The White Hart, Hook.   *(Publ: Raphael Tuck & Sons "Art" Series 1350. "In Dickens' Land." Postally unused.)*
The history of the White Hart is obscure. It is known to have existed as an "alehouse" in the 18th century, but was undoubtedly rebuilt when the road from Kingston to Leatherhead was turnpiked in 1811. It then became — as shown here — an attractive coaching inn for travellers on the new turnpike road (which became the modern A243 and dual carriageway)
Hodgson's Kingston Brewery bought the White Hart in 1884 and replaced the old building with the present one in 1930.

Clayton Road, Hook. (Approaching Claygate)   *(Publ: T.Seymour, Newsagent, Surbiton. Postally unused.)*
Clayton Road was paid for by public subscription and officially opened by the Rev. Thomas Pyne, vicar of Hook, on Sept. 23rd 1867. Part of it follows the line of a centuries-old track which petered out at what is now Devon Way. The purpose of the new road was to extend this old route so it linked with Woodstock Lane and so provided a useful short cut to Esher and Cobham.   Clayton Road, named after a prominent local family, retained its rural character until the housebuilding boom that followed the opening of Kingston By-pass in 1927. So did the rest of Hook. Kelly's directory for 1927 quotes the village population as 640 and remarks that 'the chief crops are wheat, oats, barley and fruit.'   When this picture was taken, the Moon family had Old Manor Farm, a part of which is seen here, and Alfred Pearce and Sons were running the Clayton Hand Laundry from Laurel Villa, seen on the left. This is now the site of Arbrook Lodge, a new development of retirement flats. The large house in the old picture still survives, but its personality has been totally changed by replacement windows.

SOURCES USED FOR THIS BOOK

A major source of material has been countless editions of *The Surrey Comet*, first published by Thomas Philpott in 1854 from premises in Brighton Road, Surbiton. It has appeared every week without a break since then, and is now Surrey's oldest surviving newspaper.

Another mainspring was the *Kingston and Surbiton News*, launched by William Drewett from Kingston Market Place in 1881 and continued by him until 1900, when he merged his company with that of the *Surrey Comet*.

Ordnance Survey maps, from the 1860's to the present, have been consulted at every turn, as have the local street and trade directories that were published annually for several years by Phillipsons of Kingston Market Place, and Kelly's, who operated from a converted mill to the south of Kingston's Fairfield.

Phillipson's Directory appeared from the mid-19th century to 1906, when George Phillipson died. Kelly's left Kingston in 1932, but continued to publish their Kingston and Surbiton directories until 1971. The guides formerly issued each year by Surbiton Council and Kingston Council also provided me with useful facts and figures.

All these newspapers, maps, directories and guides can be seen at Kingston Museum and Heritage Centre.

Kingston Council minutes are a good guide to why, when and where roads and other public amenities were created or improved. They can be seen, by prior appointment, at the Record Office in Surrey County Hall, Penrhyn Road, Kingston.

Other indispensable companions in this work were:

Title	Author	Publisher
Old Kingston: Recollections of an Octogenarian	G.W.Ayliffe	Surrey Comet 1914. Reprint 1972
The Story of 'Hook in Kingston'	Marion Bone	St Paul's Church, Hook. 1989
Picture Postcards and their Publishers	Anthony Byatt	Golden Age Postcard Books 1978
Half a Century of Kingston History	F.S. Merryweather	Kingston Polytechnic. Reprint 1976
Surbiton: 32 years of Local Self - Government, 1855 to 1887.	Rowley Richardson	Bull & Son, Surbiton. 1888
The Shell Book of Firsts	Patrick Robertson	Ebury Press & Michael Joseph. 1974
The Story of Kingston	June Sampson	Michael Lancet 1972
Hidden Kingston	June Sampson	Surrey Comet 1975
Guide to Kingston Old Town Conservation Area.	June Sampson	Kingston Society 1976
All Change	June Sampson	News Origin Ltd. Revised edition 1991
Kingston's Past Rediscovered	Joan Wakeford	Phillimore for KUTAS & Surrey Local History Council 1990
From Talworth Hamlet to Tolworth Tower	Patricia J. Ward	The Author. 1975
Post Cards	Martin Willoughby	Phillips Collectors' Guides 1989